Foreword

I like the idea of Quick Guides. Teachers need reliable
information and advice on a very wide range of subjects
related to their work and they need it to be accessible
and concise. This series attempts to meet those needs by
drawing on the knowledge of experienced practitioners
and presenting the essential material in a format which
facilitates rapid reference and provides valuable action
checklists.

I am sure that these guides will be useful to teachers, to
governors, to parents and indeed to all who are
concerned with the effective management of all aspects
of education.

John Sutton

General Secretary
Secondary Heads Association

Drug Education, ages 4–11: a quick guide

Janice Slough is a consultant and trainer in Personal and Social Education. She is based on the Isle of Wight, and has previously worked as a teacher, youth worker and health education co-ordinator.

Contents

Contents

Introduction

We live in a drug orientated society, where drugs are used medically and socially, legally and illegally. The same drug can cure or kill, depending on who uses it, and how it is used. It is no wonder therefore that our children are confused by all the differing messages they receive. From an early age, children are influenced by the world around them, and it is vital that from the very beginning they are encouraged to respect their bodies and exercise control over what goes into them.

Many people, including parents and, through the National Curriculum, the government, are looking to schools as a forum where drug education can play an important role in safeguarding pupils' long term health.

This publication guides schools through the steps of planning and implementing a drug education programme as part of a whole school policy for health education and promoting healthy lifestyles. It highlights the drugs and substances which primary school children will be most familiar with, and describes a drug education programme which reflects the needs and abilities of 4–11 year olds.

Introduction

This publication guides schools through five clear steps towards a whole school framework involving staff, pupils, parents and the community. Each step provides aims, ideas and information, and helps schools explore the issues which they may need to address in order to achieve a positive and relevant response to drugs.

✓ You may find it useful to tick the boxes when each task is completed.

What is a drug?

- The word 'drug' covers anything taken into the body to change it in some way. It includes medicines, alcohol and tobacco, as well as illegal drugs such as heroin or cannabis.

- Some drugs have only a physical effect on the body, such as relieving pain or fighting infection.

- Others have a psychological effect as well, in that they affect the mind or emotions.

- Many drugs which are used medically for their physical effects also have psychological ones.

- Some substances whose main use is not for their effect on the body, such as the solvents in glues, can also be used like drugs.

- Sometimes the word 'substance' is used to mean drugs and other substances which can be used like them. This can be confusing, since there are so many more substances which are not drugs and have no drug-like effects.

'A drug is a substance that alters the way in which the body functions.' *Martin Plant,* Drugs in Perspective.

Drugs and other substances familiar to primary school children

Most primary school children know more about drugs than their parents or teachers realise.

☐ Medicines: a wide variety of drugs used to treat illnesses; prescribed by a doctor or bought 'over the counter' (without prescription) from pharmacies and other shops.

☐ Caffeine: found in tea, coffee, chocolate and some soft drinks, including those marketed for young children. Giving it up can cause withdrawal symptoms such as irritability and headaches.

☐ Alcohol: on sale in many outlets in the community, and widely advertised. Used socially, especially at celebrations such as birthdays, family meals and weddings.

☐ Tobacco (usually in the form of cigarettes; contains nicotine): used socially in the home or the community, brought to children's attention through advertisements and for sale in shops.

☐ Cannabis: usually smoked with tobacco. Young children may be offered cannabis by older friends.

☐ Solvents: this term is used to cover everyday substances used in the home, garage, shed or at school, including the solvents in glues and dry cleaning fluids, as well as similar volatile substances such as aerosol propellants and lighter fuels.

☐ Berries, plants and fungi: many berries, plants or fungi which children may find growing have a psychological or physiological effect, and some can be very harmful if eaten, or even handled.

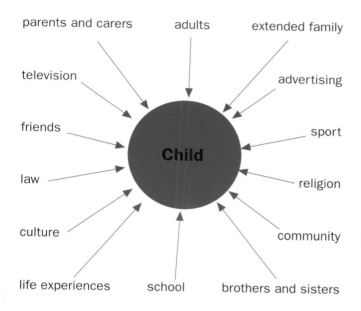

parents and carers   adults   extended family

television

advertising

friends

sport

Child

law

religion

culture

community

life experiences   school   brothers and sisters

'As they grow older, children are open to an increasingly wide range of influences and sources of information.' **Tackling Drugs Together.**

- Alcohol
  - Intoxicating, that is, alcoholic, liquor may not be given to any child under five except under medical supervision.
  - Under fourteen year olds are not allowed in the bar of licensed premises.
  - No alcohol can be sold or delivered to a person under 18.

- Tobacco
  - It is illegal to sell tobacco products to anyone under the age of sixteen.
  - It is also illegal to sell single cigarettes.

- It is illegal to share prescribed drugs with another person.

- Solvents and other volatile substances
  - Possession of solvents and sniffing are not offences. The police can only intervene if a criminal act is likely to follow.
  - It is an offence to supply a person under eighteen with a solvent-based substance if you believe it will be used for intoxication.

- Heroin, cannabis, crack, LSD, cocaine and ecstasy, as well as other drugs, such as amphetamines, which are legal if prescribed as medicines, are covered by the Misuse of Drugs Act. It is illegal to possess, grow, sell or supply them.

- It is an offence for an occupier or manager to knowingly permit cannabis to be used or supplied on their premises.

- You can take a substance away from a person in order to prevent them committing an offence. Then you should inform the police and hand over the substance or destroy it, if possible in front of a witness.

Why drug education is important in primary schools

- Children need help to equip themselves with the skills to live in a drug orientated society. The development of self esteem is a major part of drug education and helps them to maintain a healthy attitude towards drugs.
- Primary school drug education provides a forum for pupils to learn about drugs and build foundations for a healthy lifestyle.
- Children form attitudes about drug use from an early age by watching adults smoking, drinking and taking medicines.
- Alcohol and nicotine are still the most widely available and abused drugs; they cause much physical and social harm. They are also the drugs that children are most likely to experiment with.
- Drugs are an important part of modern life; many people need drugs to improve the quality of their lives and to eliminate disease and pain.
- Drug education is a vehicle for addressing myths and misconceptions concerning drugs and drug taking.
- Television, films and advertising often convey a sophisticated, exciting image of inappropriate recreational drug use.
- The illicit drug trade continues to grow; the misuse of drugs has become a serious problem in many countries.
- Volatile substances are used by young children more than other drugs and can be very dangerous.
- Drug education is part of the Science National Curriculum at Key Stages 1 and 2 (see Content of primary school drug education).
- OFSTED will monitor schools' policies for drug education and drug related incidents as part of their regular inspections.

'Teachers in primary schools have reported that their pupils already display some knowledge of drug misuse in their local communities.'
Drug Prevention and Schools.

'*A planned programme of health education is one of the ways in which schools prepare pupils for the opportunities, responsibilities and experiences of adult life.' Curriculum Guidance 5.*

'It is important to recognise... that drug prevention should be seen as a whole-school issue.' *Drug Prevention and Schools.*

Step one: Initial consultation

Aim: Exploration of drug education issues and values with all significant adults who deal with the pupils, and with the pupils themselves.

Step two: Policy development

Aim: A written policy on a whole school approach to drugs and drug education.

Step three: Planning for the curriculum

Aim: A shared understanding of what the school wants to achieve for its pupils through the drug education curriculum.

Step four: Drug education strategies in the primary curriculum

Aim: Agreement on a shared approach and methodology.

Step five: Content of the curriculum

Aim: The production of a drug education curriculum framework.

Step one: Initial consultation

Aim: A shared understanding of the aims of drug education and of what the school wants to achieve for its pupils.

Possible ways to go about this:

☐ Identify a member of staff to be the drug education co-ordinator.

☐ Circulate a discussion paper to staff, governors and parents.

☐ Hold a governors' meeting to discuss
- the need for drug education
- aims
- expectations
- rationale
- concerns

☐ Parents' meeting to explore ways of working together.

☐ Consultation with professionals, for instance the Health Education Adviser in your LEA, the police, and your local Health Promotion Unit or Service.

☐ Work with pupils to establish their perceptions, concerns and needs regarding drugs and drug issues.

The widest possible consultation is needed at the outset if drug education is to be effective.

Before beginning to plan, the school needs to decide what its philosophy, aims, and objectives are on the subject of drugs.

- What do we mean by 'drugs'?
- What concerns us about drugs?
- What are our pupils' needs and perceptions?
- What are the drug issues in the community surrounding the school?
- What drugs and substances are our pupils already familiar with?
- What do we want to achieve?
- Why do we want to address drugs and drug issues in the curriculum?
- What messages do we want to put across?
- How do we plan a comprehensive drug education programme?
- Who do we involve in the planning?
- How much finance have we available for this programme?
- What do we want the programme to look like?
- What resources and skills do we already have?
- What help is available from outside?
- How can we involve governors and parents?
- What staff training would be necessary?
- What resources will we need?
- Is drug education in the school development plan?
- How can we assess the effectiveness of the programme?

'Jugs and herrings' – the draw and write technique

A Health Education Authority project begun in 1984 produced interesting and useful research into children's perceptions of the world of drugs.

An investigative technique called Draw and Write was devised by Noreen Wetton, whereby small children could communicate their thinking on health related subjects through drawings. Those who could write added captions, or their teacher could help with this.

Over two thousand children in Nottingham and Hampshire took part in the World of Drugs Draw and Write investigation. Their responses were analysed, and key drug education messages for each age group identified. 'Jugs and Herrings' became the familiar title for the research after some children drew jugs for 'drugs' and herrings for 'heroin'.

From this research, the Health for Life materials were written (see bibliography). *Health for Life* Book 2 provides instructions for investigating four to twelve year-olds' perceptions of drugs. Many primary schools now use this technique to:

- understand their pupil's perceptions of the world of drugs.
- redress any misunderstandings, myths and incorrect information revealed during the investigation.
- identify key messages to be included in drug education.
- provide evidence for parents, governors and other interested adults about the need for drug education in primary schools.

Research shows that even small children have knowledge and ideas about drugs and drug issues.

'Your Child and Drugs'

Aim: To explore ways to develop a partnership between home and school for the benefit of our children.

- [ ] Presentation: Drugs and our children
  - influences, pressures and the community.
- [ ] What do we want for our children?
  - skills, values, qualities and attitudes.

- [ ] How can we help our children develop these?
  - sharing experiences and strategies.

- [ ] What messages do we want to give our children?

- [ ] What to do if things go wrong
  - situations
  - guidelines
  - signs and symptoms
  - where to obtain help

- [ ] Who to contact in the school or community if you are concerned about drugs.

A drug awareness programme for adults who deal with children

Purpose:

- [ ] to increase knowledge and awareness of the different kinds of drug available and how they are used.
- [ ] to raise awareness of our attitudes towards drugs and drug issues.
- [ ] to explore ways of dealing with drug misuse.
- [ ] to find out what other agencies are doing.

Content:

- [ ] definition of a drug
- [ ] the local picture of drug use
- [ ] importance of drug education for children
- [ ] facts about drugs
- [ ] use and misuse of drugs
- [ ] effects of drugs
- [ ] attitudes and values around drug use
- [ ] why people take drugs
- [ ] signs and symptoms of drug use
- [ ] defining a drug problem
- [ ] drugs and the law
- [ ] dealing with drug misuse
- [ ] local and national agencies which provide a service

'An appropriate level of training, information and guidance needs to be provided not only to the teaching staff delivering drug education but also to all other teaching and non-teaching staff involved in the school community.' **Drug Education in Schools: the need for a new impetus.**

The policy needs to involve every aspect of the school, both as an educational institution and as a community.

Aim: a written policy on a whole school approach to drugs and drug issues.

Ways to go about this:

- Appoint a committee representing staff, parents, governors and interested members of the local community to draw up a school policy on drugs and drug education.

- Explore the whole school ethos and the role of pastoral work to raise pupils' self-esteem and confidence.

- Produce guidelines for dealing with:
  - sensitive issues
  - misuse of drugs by pupils
  - confidentiality
  - child protection
  - the use of medicines in school

- Develop the concept of a Health Promoting School: identify what makes a healthy school, and set up ways of working towards the goals you identify.

- Work towards a Healthy School Award (enquire for details from your LEA Health Co-ordinator or Health Promotion Unit).

- Develop a smoke free school policy.

A specimen primary school policy on drugs and substances

Statement: All non-medical drugs on the school premises are unacceptable.

Guidelines:

Schools need a clear policy on drugs so that everyone knows what is expected of them.

☐ We recognise that adults are role models for pupils, and so we commit ourselves to:
  - providing a smoke free environment, both during the school day and at evening functions.
  - not using alcohol on the premises, or giving alcohol for prizes or raffles.
  - informing parents and visitors of what we are doing and encouraging them to support us.
  - actively seeking ways to avoid the need for over-the-counter drugs, such as a quiet room for headaches.

☐ The promise of confidentiality is not realistic, especially when there is a risk to the safety of a pupil or other people. The pupil should always be told, however, when information is to be passed on. Information concerning risk to pupils must be passed to the head teacher immediately, and she or he will consult parents and other appropriate adults.

☐ Administering medicines: Medicines can only be administered by a named person (normally the school nurse where there is one), and only at the request of parents. Parents and carers must inform him or her and hand over the medicines. The named person must record his or her possession of the medicines and the time of each administration. Only the parents and the named person may handle the medicines.

The main concern of the policy must be the welfare of the school's pupils.

A pupil suffering from the ill effects of drug use should be treated in the same way as if they had any other illness. Steps must be taken to ascertain what has been taken, and any evidence, such as tablets, packaging or vomit, must be saved.

The focus must always be on the individual pupil, not on the drug. If a pupil is at risk, or displaying risky behaviour, she or he will be treated as they would in the case of any other pastoral concern:

- each person and situation is treated according to the individual circumstances.
- parents are consulted.
- appropriate professionals, such as the Education Welfare Officer, Police, Social Services Department and health professionals are consulted.
- an action plan is devised for support, discipline and coping strategies, both immediately and in the longer term.

The school will have a comprehensive drug education programme, within the health education curriculum, which will provide pupils with appropriate knowledge, develop skills to deal with living in a drug oriented society, and explore positive attitudes and values in relation to drugs and drug issues.

Guidelines for dealing with incidents involving drugs

If a pupil is found with a drug or similarly misusable substance:

- Obtain medical help if necessary. Keep any evidence of what has been taken, such as substance, package or vomit.

- The substance should be taken away from him or her and placed in a safe container, if possible in the presence of a witness.

- The pupil or pupils should be interviewed separately.

- Notify their parents.

- Inform the police if this is considered appropriate, and follow their advice.

- Arrange whatever help the pupil needs, such as counselling from an outside agency.

- Work with the parents to agree an action plan, for example to develop self esteem or different social interests.

It is no good waiting for an incident to happen before you decide how to deal with it.

Many issues involving drugs are potentially problematic, but we must be careful that we do not avoid them on that account.

Sensitive issues that may arise in primary school drug education:

☐ Smoking amongst significant adults in the child's life. The emphasis in drug education should be on individual responsibility for one's own actions and body. Long term smoking parents are addicted, and it is not the school's business to condemn their behaviour. However, teachers and other adults can provide positive role models.

☐ Misuse of drugs at home. Parents who are misusing alcohol or illegal drugs will inevitably affect their children. The school should monitor the situation, and consult with such people as the Education Welfare Officer, Child Protection Team and, if there is firm evidence of misuse of illegal drugs, the police.

☐ The influence of older children. Pupils need to develop and practice such skills as assertion, coping with negative pressure, and dealing with conflict. This can be done through Personal and Social Education, drama, discussion and assemblies.

☐ Objections to giving information to children 'as it might excite their curiosity'. Primary schools especially may encounter this criticism. Please refer to 'Why drug education is important in a primary school' and 'Jugs and Herrings', which will help counter these objections.

Guidelines for dealing with sensitive issues (continued)

Pressure to sensationalise the issue of drugs with a 'shock horror' approach, 'to frighten children into not taking them'. This type of approach is known to be ineffective except in the immediate short term, but schools can come under pressure from well meaning groups or individuals to take such a simplistic approach, and it can be tempting to go for obvious evidence of 'something being done'. However, effective drug education takes time and a thorough exploration of the issues. It is also important to avoid frightening young children, who can worry in secret about information they do not understand properly. Information evenings for parents and other interested adults can be used to explain the school's point of view.

Pupils disclosing information about drug misuse by people they know. Before encouraging discussion in class, the teacher should explain the school's policy on confidentiality, that is that any information regarding harm to self or others, or illegal acts, will have to be passed on.

Teachers and schools may have to exercise a good deal of tact and judgement in balancing the different interests and viewpoints involved in drug issues.

Schools have a responsibility to provide a model of a non-smoking lifestyle for their pupils.

Tobacco smoking is the cause of much ill health and death, in both smokers and passive smokers (those who breathe other people's smoke). It is an important health issue for all adults and children who use our school. Everyone has the right to breathe clean air, and adults have a responsibility to make sure children enjoy this right and can look to non-smoking role models.

Aims:

- to provide a smoke free environment for our pupils.
- to guarantee adult non-smokers the right to work in a smoke free environment.
- to encourage and help staff and pupils to give up smoking.
- to help staff and pupils not to start smoking.

Implementation:

- Smoking is not allowed on school premises, including the school grounds (if schools wish to designate a smoking area, it should be somewhere not used by pupils, such as a small room off the staff room).
- Smoking is not allowed at evening functions; this must be agreed by outside bodies hiring rooms.
- All potential new members of staff must be informed of the policy, and agree to abide by it.
- Visitors will be informed of the policy when they arrive. Signs will also be displayed around the school.
- Help will be provided for any member of staff or pupil who wishes to give up smoking, in co-operation with the school nurse and health promotion staff.
- The smoking policy will be reinforced by promotion at parents' evenings and on occasions such as National No Smoking Day.

Step three: Planning for the curriculum

Aim:

A clear idea of what the school wants to achieve for its pupils through the drug education curriculum.

Ways to achieve this:

☐ Staff meetings to:

- consider the aims of primary school drug education.
- discuss good practice in drug education.
- explore ways of incorporating drug education into the curriculum.

Careful planning will ensure effective drug education.

The school must be clear about what it wants to achieve through drug education before it can decide how to go about it.

'The essential aim should be to give pupils the facts, emphasise the benefits of a healthy lifestyle, and give young people the knowledge and skills to make informed and responsible choices now and later in life.' *Drug Prevention and Schools.*

The main aims of primary drug education are to:

- [ ] encourage a healthy respect for all substances taken into the body.

- [ ] raise pupils' awareness of the world of drugs so that they can make informed decisions about their own drug use.

- [ ] enable pupils to explore their own attitudes towards drugs and drug issues.

- [ ] promote a no smoking lifestyle amongst pupils.

- [ ] enable each pupil to develop confidence and self-esteem.

- [ ] develop skills to enable pupils to live and cope in a drug orientated society.

- [ ] promote an awareness that drugs are neither good or bad in themselves, and that all substances can be harmful if not used properly.

- [ ] develop responsibility towards themselves and each other.

Good practice in drug education

☐ Drug education is part of a whole school approach to the health education of each pupil.

☐ Drug education concerns both legal and illegal drugs, and drugs taken socially or used as medicines, bought over the counter or on prescription. It should also include substances such as solvents and plants which, while not strictly drugs, are used in similar ways.

☐ The focus should be on the person who is taking or might be taking the drugs rather than the drugs themselves.

☐ Drug education can never be achieved by a one-off course. It needs to be carefully planned and progress with pupils' understanding. 'Teaching about illegal drugs is unlikely to have any lasting effect if a lesson is given in isolation or as a one-off response to a drug related incident in the school.' *Drug Prevention and Schools.*

☐ When planning drug education, the following should be taken into consideration:
- the maturity of the pupils
- pupils' needs
- community values and concerns
- religious and cultural factors
- the expertise of the staff

☐ Children need the knowledge to make informed choices, skills to help resist negative pressures and develop positive lifestyles, and values to help them respect themselves and others. Drug education is therefore about the acquisition of knowledge, the development of skills and the exploration of attitudes and values.

Drug education must be approached sensitively and be based on sound information.

If drug education is to be effective, the adults concerned with it must be in agreement about the best ways to approach it.

Aim:

Agreement on a shared approach and methodology

Possible ways to go about this:

☐ Drug awareness training for staff, governors and parents.

☐ Staff training and discussion on:

- drug education for the primary school child.
- different approaches to drug education.
- a cross-curricular approach to developing self-esteem.
- classroom methodology for developing skills and exploring attitudes.
- dealing with sensitive issues.

A drug education training programme for staff and governors

Purpose:

- to provide a common base of knowledge and expertise and the confidence to deliver drug education.

- to agree common aims, principles and messages for drug education.

- to explore the effectiveness of drug education.

- to disseminate appropriate teaching resources.

- to plan work for the curriculum.

- to explore the school's and the individual teacher's responsibility and role in specific drug related situations.

Content:

- the needs of our pupils

- the rationale, aims, principles of drug education

- the messages we want to put across

- different approaches to drug education

- the National Curriculum and drug education

- where drug education fits into the curriculum

- resources and materials

- planning a programme

- sensitive issues

- guidelines for drug related incidents

'Teachers delivering drug education need to have the confidence to deliver consistent and clear messages about drugs.' **Drug Education in Schools: the need for a new impetus.**

'It is widely
recognised that the
provision and
acquisition of
information alone is
unlikely to promote
healthy, or
discourage
unhealthy
behaviour.'
Curriculum
Guidance 5.

As pupils vary, so does the impact of drug education on them. Schools should therefore consider a variety of teaching approaches. 'The best programmes combine several approaches and should contain material on peer influences and refusal skills.' Reginald Smart, 'Window of Opportunity' Congress, Australia 1991.

Children's ability to handle information and ideas changes as they grow older. Drug education should therefore progress through the pupil's school career, reinforcing previous learning.

The 'shock horror' approach can be tempting as it is quick and didactic and can be entertaining for the pupils; however, it is rarely effective in the long term. It can also be frightening for small children, who may become worried that friends or parents are going to die.

A judgemental attitude from a teacher does not allow the pupils to formulate their own opinions and could suffocate a learning atmosphere. Nevertheless, the children's welfare is always the most important consideration.

Information alone is unlikely to encourage healthy behaviour. Skills based lessons where pupils participate in making decisions, solving problems, negotiation and role-play are essential in changing behaviour and developing values.

Audio-visual aids, visits, games, drama, art, surveys, questionnaires and all kinds of different activities can provide variety and interest in developing the pupil's understanding and learning.

Using outside expertise

Many organisations and individuals both nationally and locally are most concerned about the misuse of drugs. Preventive education, especially in schools where there is easy access to young people, is seen as a vital way of stemming the tide of illicit drug use. Schools are often approached by people or organisations who offer their time and expertise in making a contribution to drug education. These may be health visitors, school nurses, health education or promotion officers, members of local drug prevention teams, police officers, prison officers, ex-users, or representatives from religious organisations. If their help is taken up by schools, it is important that they are seen as part and, not all, of the school's drug education and that their visit is in line with the school's approach to drugs and drug education.

It is also important that the school asks the following:

- The purpose of the visit and the expected results.
- Details of what will be included in the session.
- What the context of the visit will be within the existing curriculum.
- What the content and approach will be in relation to the pupil's maturity, needs and experience.
- What the visitor can offer which cannot be provided by the school.
- Does the visitor have experience in working with primary age children? Make sure she or he is not going to frighten them.
- What other schools have received these visits and how they have felt about the effectiveness of the session.
- What the role of the school staff will be during the visit.

'Schools need to be aware of the range of agencies and services available in their area, including primary healthcare services, which can help in developing the school drug education programme.'
Drug Education in Schools: the need for a new impetus.

'Many schools will find that visiting speakers can make a valuable contribution to a planned and co-ordinated programme of health education.'
Drug Misuse and the Young: a Guide for the Education Service.

Visitors from outside organisations can have a great deal to offer, for example:

- different experiences
- specialised knowledge
- a change of face and perspective
- no preconceived ideas about individual pupils
- a support system for school staff
- a reinforcement of the school's messages about drugs
- a model for future work by school staff
- community links
- an opportunity for pupils to prepare for and look after a visitor

Step five: Content of the primary school drug education curriculum

Aim: the production of a drug education curriculum framework.

Possible ways to go about this:

☐ A curriculum audit to ascertain what is already being covered.

☐ A working party to produce a framework for drug education.

☐ Adding elements of drug education to existing topics. It can be included in the context of healthy living, work on the human body, or safety in the home and environment.

☐ Drug education can be included in special 'bolt-on' programmes of work and activities, such as Health Week.

☐ Including drug education as part of the development of personal and social skills.

The primary school drug education curriculum needs to be well co-ordinated with the rest of the school's work.

'Health Education
covers the provision
of information about
what is good and
what is harmful and
involves the
development of
skills which will
help, individuals to
use their knowledge
effectively.'
Curriculum
Guidance 5.

Knowledge:

- what a drug is
- effects of drugs
- different kinds of drugs
- use and misuse of drugs
- risk taking
- substances in the home, countryside and school
- alcohol, nicotine and solvents
- medicines and their uses
- people who handle drugs at work
- people who need drugs to live
- drugs and the law
- people who can help us with problems

Skills:

- self esteem
- assertiveness
- communication
- coping with conflict
- coping with responses from other people
- problem solving
- developing positive relationships
- keeping safe
- dealing with loss
- resisting peer pressure
- dealing with stress
- knowing where to go for help

Values and Attitudes:

- respect and responsibility for oneself and others
- accepting things from strangers and friends
- socially acceptable drugs
- drugs and sport
- smoking in public places
- why people misuse drugs
- what counts as misuse

What the National Curriculum Science Order says about primary drug education

The new National Curriculum Science Order prescribes the following learning objectives for drug education in primary schools:

Key Stage One (ages 5–7)

- [ ] to know about the role of drugs as medicines.

Key Stage Two (ages 7–11)

- [ ] to relate their understanding of science to their personal health.
- [ ] to understand that tobacco, alcohol and other drugs can have harmful effects.

The government recognises the need for drug education in primary schools as part of a national strategy for the prevention of drug abuse.

National Curriculum Guidance 5: Health Education has the following suggestions for primary school education on substance use and misuse.

Key Stage One

☐ Know that all medicines are drugs but not all drugs are medicines.

☐ Know that all substances can be harmful if not use properly.

☐ Know about different medicines and that some people need them to live a normal life.

☐ Know and understand simple safety rules about medicines, tablets, solvents and other household substances.

Key Stage Two

☐ Know that all medicines are drugs but not all drugs are medicines.

☐ Know that there are over-the-counter and prescribed, legal and illegal substances and have some understanding of their effects.

☐ Know how to make simple choices and exercise some basic techniques for resisting pressure from friends and others.

☐ Know the important and beneficial part which drugs have played in society.

Outline of a primary school topic on drugs and safety

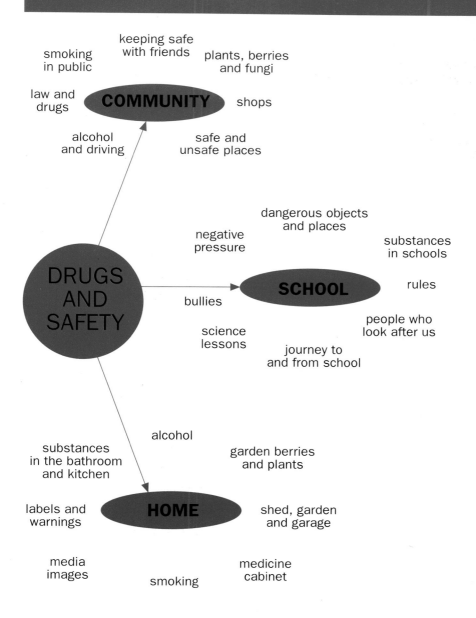

'*Given its prevalence, alcohol raises particular concerns in relation to its use by pupils of primary age.*'
Drug Prevention and Schools.

Primary school teaching on alcohol could cover:

- what is alcohol?
- the history of alcohol
- the various ways alcohol is used, for instance in perfumes
- different kinds of alcohol
- different strengths of alcohol
- units of alcohol
- reading labels to assess strengths
- alcohol and advertising
- why people drink alcohol
- what alcohol does to the body
- safe and sensible limits
- driving a car and alcohol
- alcohol and the law
- non-alcoholic alternatives
- what to do if...
- where to seek help

Education about smoking

This could include some of the following topics:

- [ ] what is nicotine?
- [ ] the history of smoking
- [ ] why people smoke
- [ ] effects on the body and on other people
- [ ] helping people to stop smoking
- [ ] smoking and the law
- [ ] smoking and advertising
- [ ] smoking and breathing
- [ ] the rights of smokers and non-smokers
- [ ] resisting pressures to smoke
- [ ] smoking in pregnancy
- [ ] passive smoking

Tobacco smoking remains the largest preventable cause of death.

Education about solvents
(volatile substance misuse)

These topics could be covered:

- dangerous substances in the home, school and environment

- labels and warnings

- what are solvents?

- effects of solvents on the body

- good and bad uses of solvents

- solvents and the law

- what to do if...
  - a friend was sniffing
  - you were offered solvents to sniff
  - you found someone unconscious
  - an accident happened

- resisting pressure

- problem solving

- personal safety

Education about other drugs

These are the essential topics for primary school children to learn about:

- What is a drug?

- Different kinds of drugs: medicines, legal and illegal, social, used in sport, and so on.

- The names of drugs.

- The effects of drugs: what happens to our minds and bodies.

- Why people take drugs.

- How to resist peer pressure.

- Problem solving.

- Where to go for help.

Children may come across illegal drugs at any time; the more they know, the better they'll be able to cope.

DRUGS: the acrostic

D rugs are substances taken into the body to cause physical or psychological changes.

R ight from an early age, children are influenced by family, friends, community and the media.

U nless adults act as positive role models, children receive confusing messages about drugs.

G ood drug education is planned and progressive, and responds to pupils' needs and concerns.

S chools' role is vital in providing effective drug education and dealing with drug related incidents.

ADFAM National
(family support and self-help)
5th floor, Epworth House
25 City Road
London EC1Y 1AA
telephone 0171-638 3700

Alcohol Concern
Waterbridge House
32–36 Loman Street
London SW7 0EE
telephone 0171-928 7377

ASH (Action on Smoking and Health)
109 Gloucester Place
London W1H 4EJ
telephone 0171-935 3519

Health Publications Unit
(free leaflets etc.)
DSS Distribution Centre
Heywood Stores
Manchester Road
Heywood
Lancashire OL10 2PZ
telephone 0800 555 777 (free)

Doping Control Unit
The Sports Council
3–10 Melton Street
London NW1 2EB
telephone 0171-383 5667

Drugs in School
telephone 01345 366666
Helpline 10am–5pm Mon–Fri
all calls charged at local rate.
A confidential service for pupils,
parents and staff concerned about
drug incidents in school.

Health Education Authority
Hamilton House
Mabledon Place
London WC1H 9TX
telephone 0171-383 3833

Health Wise
9 Slater Street
Liverpool L1 4BW
telephone 0151-707 2262

Institute for the Study of Drug
Dependence
Waterbridge House
32–36 Loman Street
London SE1 0EE
telephone 0171-928 1211
(publications)

Narcotics Anonymous
UK Service Office
PO Box 1980
London N19 3LS
telephone 0171-281 9933 (recording
about local meetings)
helpline 0171-498 9005
office 0171-272 9040

National AIDS Helpline
0800 567 123 (free)

National Drugs Helpline
0800 776600 (free)
A confidential service which offers
advice, information and support about
drugs and solvents to callers
throughout the UK. The service is
funded by the Department of Health
and is open 24 hours a day all the year
round.

National Alcohol Helpline
0171-332 0202

QUIT
Victory House
170 Tottenham Court Road
London W1P 0HA
telephone 0171-487 2858

Release
(legal and welfare problems)
388 Old Street
London EC1V 9LT
telephone 0171-729 9904
emergency helpline 0171-603 8654

Re-Solv
(solvent misuse problems)
30a High Street
Stone
Staffordshire ST15 8AW
telephone 01785 817885

Scottish Drugs Forum
5 Oswald Street
Glasgow G1 4QR
telephone 0141-221 1175

Standing Council on Drug Abuse
(SCODA)
Waterbridge House
32-6 Loman Street
London SE1 0EE
telephone 0171-928 9500

TACADE
1 Hulme Place
The Crescent
Salford
Greater Manchester M5 4QA
telephone 0161-745 8925

Welsh Office Drugs Unit
Cathays Park
Cardiff CF1 3NQ
telephone 01222 825111

Julian Cohen, Sue Scott, Norman Scott and James Kay, *The Primary Schools Drugs Pack*, Healthwise 1995.

Curriculum Guidance 5: Health Education, National Curriculum Council 1990.

Drug Education in Schools: the need for a new impetus, a report by the Advisory Council on the Misuse of Drugs, HMSO 1993.

Drug Misuse and the Young: a guide for the education service, Department for Education 1992.

Drug Prevention and Schools, Circular 4/95, Department for Education.

John Lloyd and Ron Morton, *Health Education*, Key Stages 1 and 2 (teacher resource book and photocopiable pupil activities, including medicines and drugs), Blueprints Series, Stanley Thornes 1992.

Alysoun Moon, *Skills for the Primary School Child* (1 and 2) (skill based lessons and activities based on personal safety), TACADE 1990.

Martin Plant, *Drugs in Perspective*, Hodder and Stoughton 1987.

Tackling Drugs Together: a consultation document on a strategy for England 1995–1998, HMSO 1994.

Noreen Wetton, *Health for Life: a teacher's planning guide to health education in the primary school* ('The World of Drugs', 'Keeping Myself Safe' and 'Me and My Relationships'), Thomas Nelson and Sons 1989.

Trefor Williams, Noreen Wetton and Alysoun Moon, *A Way In: a description of the Draw and Write research*, Health Education Authority 1989.

Trefor Williams, Noreen Wetton and Alysoun Moon, *A Picture of Health: what do you do that makes you healthy and keeps you healthy?* Health Education Authority 1989.

Drug Education, ages 4–11: a quick guide

Related titles from Folens

Solvents, Drugs and Young People:
a cross-curricular approach
Richard Ives and Barbara Wyvill
ISBN 1 85467 181 2

AlcoholFacts A
Dr Gerald Beales
ISBN 1 85467 232 0

SmokingFacts A
Dr Gerald Beales
ISBN 1 85467 221 5

Understanding Your Body
Anne Wilkes
ISBN 1 85467 206 1

Understanding Drugs 2nd edition
Ian Harvey
ISBN 1 85467 184 7

Raising Self–Esteem: 50 activities
Murray White
ISBN 1 85467 231 2

Self–Esteem, Its Meaning and Value in Schools,
A and B
Murray White
ISBN 1 85467 253 3 and 1 85467 263 0

Folens resource packs are:

✓ **Fully photocopiable**

✓ **Ready for use**

✓ **Flexible**

✓ **Clearly designed**

✓ **Tried and tested**

✓ **Cost-effective**

Quick Guides are up to date, stimulating and readable A5 books, packed with essential information and key facts on important issues in education

Health education

Drugs Education for children aged 4–11: A Quick Guide
Janice Slough
ISBN 1 85467 326 2

Drugs Education for children aged 11–18: A Quick Guide
Janice Slough
ISBN 1 85467 324 6

Alcohol: A Quick Guide
Dr Gerald Beales
ISBN 1 85467 300 9

Smoking Issues: A Quick Guide
Paul Hooper
ISBN 1 85467 309 2

Sex Education: A Quick Guide for Teachers
Dr Michael Kirby
ISBN 1 85467 228 2

Sex Education for children aged 4–11: A Quick Guide for parents and carers
Janice Slough
ISBN 1 85467 312 2

Sex Education for children aged 11–18: A Quick Guide for parents and carers
Janice Slough
ISBN 1 85467 313 0

Career enhancement

Assertiveness: A Quick Guide
Chrissie Hawkes-Whitehead
ISBN 1 85467 305 X

Counselling: A Quick Guide
Chrissie Hawkes-Whitehead
and Cherry Eales
ISBN 1 85467 302 5

Problem People and How to Handle Them: A Quick Guide
Ursula Markham
ISBN 1 85467 317 3

Class and school management

Bullying: A Quick Guide
Dr Carrie Herbert
ISBN 1 85467 323 8

School Inspections: A Quick Guide
Malcolm Massey
ISBN 1 85467 308 4

Grief, Loss and Bereavement: A Quick Guide
Penny Casdagli & Francis Gobey
ISBN 1 85467 307 6

Safety on Educational Visits: A Quick Guide
Michael Evans
ISBN 1 85467 306 8

Equal Opportunities: A Quick Guide
Gwyneth Hughes & Wendy Smith
ISBN 1 85467 303 3

Working in Groups: A Quick Guide
Pauline Maskell
ISBN 1 85467 304 1

Organising Conferences and Events: A Quick Guide
David Napier
ISBN 1 85467 314 9

Working with Parents: A Quick Guide
Dr Michael Kirby
ISBN 1 85467 315 7

For further information

For further details of any of our publications mentioned in this Quick Guide, please fill in and post this form (or a photocopy) to:

Folens Publishers　　　　　　Tel: 01582 472788
Albert House　　　　　　　　Fax: 01582 472575
Apex Business Centre
Boscombe Road
Dunstable LU5 4RL

Name ....

Job Title ....

Organisation ....

Address ....

....

Postcode ....

Tel No. ....

Fax No. ....

☐　　**Please send me details of the following publications:**

Notes

Notes

Drug Education, ages 4–11: a quick guide

Notes

Notes

Drug Education, ages 4–11: a quick guide

THE
FARM
BUSINESS